How to Buy and Sell Gold & Silver Privately

Must Know Strategies to Keep Your Portfolio Private, Stay in the IRS's Good Graces, Know Your Tax Requirements, File the Right Reports, Buy The Right Types Of Gold And Silver And Avoid Other Forms Of Metals Like The Plague

DOYLE SHULER

Table of Contents

Introduction

Congratulations on taking some of your valuable time to learn this important information. It's very smart of you to do and I commend you for that. In fact, this could be one of the most important books you will read because it could have such an important impact on your finances. One of the reasons I finally decided to stop and write this book is because I got tired of answering the same questions over and over.

I continue to be amazed at how much misinformation there is out there. Even among some pretty smart and pretty wealthy people, there seems to be some wide disagreement over many of the issues we will review in this book. So, my goal here is to set the record straight, give you all of the "working" information you need to be an educated and successful precious metals investor.

As I am sure you know, given the current state of economic affairs for both the United States and the world, precious metals are now one of the most important investments you can make. However, it's critical that you do it right. You may consider this book to be your instruction manual. As I'm sure you know, it's always smart to "read the manual" *before* you get started. Right?

Here is my promise to you. I know your time is very valuable and I will not waste it here by going on and on, into the minute details of every little possible facet of precious metals investing. That would bore me and I'm sure it would likely bore you as well. I will keep this pretty much "high level" information so that you can consume it pretty fast, and then start your precious metals journey. Sound good? Great.

Lastly, over decades of metals investing I have discovered the good programs, the bad programs and the ugly programs. At the end of this book you will find a **Resource** section that has a number of programs that I have discovered over the years that deserve an A+ and I wanted to share them with you so that hopefully they will save you a lot of time, money and frustration.

With that said, let's begin.

Why All of the Confusion?

There is so much confusion and misinformation in the marketplace about how the US tax laws apply to buying and selling gold and silver coins, bars and various forms of bullion. Almost every day people ask me questions like:

1. When I buy gold and silver, do I have to report the purchase, or is my purchase reported to the government?

2. Are my purchases of gold and silver taxable?

3. When I sell my gold and silver, do I have to report the sale to the IRS, or is the sale of my metals reported to the government?

4. Do I have to pay taxes on my profits when I sell my metals?

5. Can my purchases and sales of precious metals be totally confidential and private so that no one knows about them?

Do you wonder why it can be so confusing? Well, there are a few reasons below that will make perfect since to you.

The Government

Have you ever seen anything that the Government was involved with that was not confusing? All you have to do is look at the US Tax Code to know that. Well, like most everything else, the government regulates certain aspects of precious metals. If you really dig through all of the legalese and details within the law, you will find lots of "grey" areas and situations that are left up to interpretation. In fact, it is not uncommon for different precious metal's broker/dealers to have different interpretations of the exact same issue.

The Broker/Dealers

I have the upmost respect for most of the precious metals broker/dealers out there. Most of them are great companies with great people and they try to do things right and keep their customer's best interest in mind. However, just like any other industry, the precious metals industry seems to have more than its' fair share of people who put their own personal interest above their customer's interest. Consequently some of them will *"bend the truth"* about some of the issues we will discuss here.

The reason they bend the truth is obviously so they can sell you items that they make a higher profit on. So if someone were to tell you not to buy a certain item because the purchase of that item is reportable to the government, or when you go to sell it, you have to report it, you may then be influenced to buy the item they are recommending to you... which just happens to be an item they make a whole lot more profit on.

How do you protect yourself from being lied to and taken advantage of? Easy. Just learn the rules contained in this book and you will be armed with all of the information you need. You will then know when "they" are telling you the truth, and when "they" are trying to put one over on you. You can now be an educated and informed buyer!

Start With a Plan

Like anything worthwhile in life, it's always best to start with a plan. The good news is, it's actually not that complicated. However it's very important that you know the facts up front, <u>before</u> you start making your purchases. So many people seem to do the; "Ready, Fire, Aim" program and end up regretting it later. Trust me, it's much wiser to take a little bit of time up front, arm yourself with the right information, and then do the; "Ready, Aaaaimmmm….. Fire" program. So you are doing the right thing by reading this right now!

After reading this you will be very well prepared to make knowledgeable, informed and wise decisions about buying and selling your precious metals. You will do it correctly, with your goals in mind, right from the start.

Planning Your Exit Strategy In Advance

The first thing I suggest people do is to stop and ask themselves WHY they are buying physical precious metals in the first place. Are you buying to hold on to them forever, to make a quick profit, to hold on to for possible barter in the future, or to protect your assets from the rapidly devaluing dollar, or what? There are a multitude of reasons for buying precious metals and you should know your reasons before you start buying. When you discover your answer to this question, it should have a great deal of influence on what types and forms of metals that you purchase.

If you're like most people buying gold and silver these days, eventually you probably plan to at least sell some of your holdings at some time in the future. Hopefully that will be when the metals prices are sky-high, and you can "cash in" and claim some excellent profits.

PRIVACY

Privacy is a HUGE issue with most metals investors. Precious metals can be one of the most private investments that you can make. In fact, the privacy and confidentially that owning precious metals offers, is one of the biggest motivations that many investors have for buying the metals in the first place. That's all the more reason why you need to have a sound plan… in advance… so you can do everything possible to insure that your privacy is protected to the level you want it to be, now and in the future.

In order for you to keep your precious metals investments as private as possible, you must know the laws of the land, the IRS guidelines, and adhere to them. Let's take a look at the current laws and discover the key elements you need to know to maintain maximum privacy. (Note: This book details the current rules, laws and guidelines that were available at the time this book was written. As you know, new laws get passed every day and laws do change from time to time. It's wise to double check and make sure these same laws apply at the time you make your investment decisions.)

The Rules for
Buying Precious Metals

You're going to love this. This is the easy part. The simple answer is, the PURCHASES of gold and silver in the United States are <u>NOT REPORTABLE</u> to the IRS. It does not matter which broker / dealer you purchase from. There are no IRS forms to report your purchases and thus, they Do Not report any of your purchases to the IRS in any way, shape or form.

You can purchase ANY forms of gold and silver bullion that you want, (coins, bars, rounds, etc.), in ANY quantities you wish, and the <u>purchase</u> is not reportable to the IRS, neither by the dealer selling you the metals, nor by the buyer (you) who purchases the metals.

The amazing part is, no one cares how much you buy, not even the government. It's true. If you go out and buy 50 million dollars' worth of precious metals, it's still not reportable to the IRS.

That's one of the great things about this Country, you are free to buy all of the gold and silver you wish to. Now how refreshing is that? Plenty I'd say.

Buying With Cash

Believe it or not, even in the current down economy, there are still plenty of people with lots of cold hard cash. In fact, there's lots and lots of it. More and more every-day people are starting to turn those little green pieces of paper with dead presidents on them into something of real and lasting value…precious metals. After all, with our government printing new paper dollars day and night, as fast as they can, surely the value of those dollars has to go down at some point. It's simple economics.

In fact, the US Dollar has decreased in value over 96% from when the Federal Reserve first started producing them! Many smart investors aren't just sitting around waiting to see what's going to happen. They are turning some of their fiat paper dollars into physical precious metals as a store of value and wealth that has proved itself for thousands of years.

Even in this age of credit cards, online bill pay and online banking, it never ceases to amaze me how many people have so much actual cash. Especially when it comes to buying gold and silver, the cash just seems to come out of the woodwork!

When buying precious metals, many people often get the non-reporting issue mixed up between actually buying the precious metals themselves, and how they pay for them. These can be two totally and completely different issues if you are paying by cash. I'm sure you have heard something about the $10,000 reporting rule, right? This is how it works.

If you use real cash, actual green paper US dollars, to buy your metals with; if the purchase amount is over ten thousand dollars, or if you make two or more related transactions totaling ten thousand or more in cash or cash equivalents, your dealer will require you to complete a Federal Form 8300. (You can see a copy of Form 8300 in the Forms Chapter at the back of this book.)

This form requires things like your name, address, and social security number, and more. Form 8300 is the real deal and presents serious legal consequences for both the buyer and the broker/dealer seller if the form is not accurately completed and submitted, so don't take this lightly.

So, let's be clear here. It's okay to buy more than $10,000 worth of precious metals with actual cold hard paper cash. No problem at all. But if you do, the thing to be clear on is, the broker/dealer who sells you the metals must report the actual cash transaction... but they are NOT required to report the precious metals transaction. There is a big difference here.

Before you get down in the dumps over this, there is an easy solution. If you want to purchase large amounts of precious metals and don't want to have to submit a Form 8300, use a bank wire or check. Banks don't report them and precious metals dealers aren't required to either. Bank wires are easy to send and are pretty inexpensive.

Just so there is no confusion, you can purchase ANY forms of precious metals you want, and ANY amount of precious metals you want, and as long as you pay by check or bank wire, there are NO broker/dealer reporting requirements for your precious metals transaction at all. However, if you choose to pay with cash, and the purchase amount exceeds $10,000, the broker/dealer whom you are buying from must report the cash transaction itself, but they do not need to report the actual purchase of the metals.

What Does The Government Consider "Cash Equivalents"

Cash equivalents can be any form of value that that ends up being the equivalent of cash. Cash equivalents need to be readily convertible to cash, short term and highly liquid. Equivalents could be money orders, cashier's checks, treasury bills, bank CDs, money market instruments, commercial paper, marketable securities, etc.

Here is an example. If a buyer makes one purchase that totals over $10,000 and pays for it with a number of smaller payments in the form of money orders, cashier's checks, cash amounts, etc., and the total exceeds $10,000, then it IS a reportable transaction because the buyer used cash equivalents exceeding $10,000.

What Does The Government Consider "Related Transactions"?

The next question that always comes up is, how long must you wait between cash transactions for them not to be considered "related transactions?" The law is not specific as to an allowable time frame between cash transactions so this lack of clarity makes decisions difficult. Different broker/dealers will likely interpret time limits differently. You may want to ask the broker whom you are planning on buying from. They should be able to tell you what they consider to be an acceptable time period between purchases.

Some creative buyers try to get around this rule by combining payments. For example, if a buyer makes one purchase for a total of $17,000 and thinks they can get around the ruling by giving the broker/dealer $9,000 in cash and a check for $8,000, it does not work. Or in another example, a man and his wife, or a man and his "friend," go in and try to buy $12,000 worth of metals with cash, and claim that they each are individuals and they each put in $6,000 separately so they should avoid the reporting rule. They are still considered related transactions.

Sorry, but these creative approaches raise all kinds of red flags and simply do not work. The broker/dealer is still required to complete the form and report these cash transactions to the IRS or they will be found in violation of the ten thousand dollar cash rule.

Suspicious Activity Report

Yep, there is even a report called an SAR or Suspicious Activity Report. This law went largely unnoticed until the 9/11 attacks. Following the attacks the US Government rewrote many federal regulations and introduced the USA Patriot Act.

Under the SAR provision the US Government requires **financial institutions** (and yes that does include coin dealers) to report transactions that either are suspicious or that even appear to be suspicious. Like many laws, there are not clear and don't clearly defined time periods and activities that are in question. The law is not specific as to an allowable time frame between cash transactions and so this lack of clarity makes decisions difficult.

The bottom line here is, don't try to beat the system. You will have to use your best judgment in these cases. Just learn and follow the rules the best you can. After all, you are buying precious metals to make your life better... not worse. If you want to stay off of the radar, don't do things that will make you pop-up on the radar. Be smart and follow the rules.

If you want to keep your purchases completely PRIVATE, then don't make any purchases with cash of over $10,000 at a time and you'll be fine... and stay private!

Do You Have To Pay
Sales Tax When Buying

The answer to this question is, *"well, it depends."* It depends on which state you live in and where you buy your precious metals from. In the states that have sales taxes on bullion, usually purchases over a certain amount are exempt. There is a chart below that will help. Please keep in mind that these laws can and do change so it will always be best to check with a local, reputable coin dealer and they will know exactly what the state tax situation is where you live. Also, keep in mind that some of these taxes are state wide, and others vary by county.

If you live in a state that charges sales tax, and you order your metals online from an out-of-state company, the company will most likely NOT charge you sales tax. However there is a chance that you will be expected to pay the "use tax" in your state. For this reason, many metals buyers buy their metals from out of state online dealers and save the state sales tax cost. To find out if you will be expected to pay a use tax, just ask your online dealer.

Below is a list of tax and non-tax states for precious metals. Please keep in mind that states can easily make changes to these laws at any time. This list will likely change so be sure to check in your area before you buy.

States that **DO** collect sales tax on precious metals bullion: Alabama, Arkansas, Washington DC, Hawaii, Indiana, Kansas, Kentucky, Maine, Minnesota, Nebraska, New Hampshire, New Jersey, New Mexico, North Carolina, Ohio, Oklahoma, Tennessee, Vermont, Virginia, West Virginia, Wisconsin, and Wyoming.

States that **DO NOT** collect sales tax on precious metals bullion: Arizona, Delaware, Georgia, Idaho, Illinois, Iowa, Michigan, Mississippi, Missouri, North Dakota, Oregon, Pennsylvania, Rhode Island, South Carolina, South Dakota, Utah, and Washington.

States that **DO** collect sales tax on precious metals bullion but have exemptions over a certain amount: California ($1,500), Connecticut ($1,000), Florida ($500), Louisiana ($1,000), Maryland ($1,000), Massachusetts ($1,000), New York ($1,000), and Texas ($1,000).

States that **VARY** based on city or county (no state tax): Alaska, Montana, and Colorado.

Summary of states that *vary* based on city or county (no state tax): Alaska, Montana, Colorado.

Arizona	Not taxed	42-5061(A)(21)
California	Taxed up to $1,500	South African coins are always taxed (e.g. Krugerrands). California Gold medallions are not taxed. Regulation 1599.
Connecticut	Taxed up to $1,000	Conn. Gen. Stat. § 12-412(45)
Florida	Taxed under $500	212.08 (7)(ww)
Georgia	Not taxed	Title 48, Section 48-8-3 (66)
Idaho	Not taxed	Title 63 Chapter 36 (63-3622V)
Indiana	Taxed	Information Bulletin #50, December 2002
Kansas	Taxed	Regulation Number 92-19-56
Louisiana	Taxed up to $1,000	RS 47:301 Chapter 2 Section 301 (16)(b)(ii)
Massachusetts	Taxed up to $1,000	Chapter 64H Section 6 (ll)
Missouri	Not Taxed	Chapter 144 Section 144.815
New York	Taxed up to $1,000	Section 1115(a)(27)
North Dakota	Not taxed	57-39.2-04.31
Oklahoma	Taxed	710 65-13-95 exempts bullion stored at a recognized depository.
Rhode Island	Not taxed	Title 44, Chapters 18-19.
South Carolina	Not taxed	Section 12-36-2120 (70)(a)
South Dakota	Not taxed	10-45-110
Tennessee	Taxed	Attorney General Opinion #12-110, December 2012
Washington	Not Taxed	WAC 458-20-248
Wisconsin	Taxed	Tax 11.78 (1)(g)

Reminder: It's important to remember to keep all of your purchase receipts when you buy gold and silver so that you will be able to keep up with your capital gains or losses. There's more to come on this later on.

When It's Time To Sell

Now that we've covered the key issues involved with buying precious metals, let's take a look at the issues involved when selling precious metals. **Note…Please do not skip over this section until you get ready to sell.** Understanding the issues involved when selling your metals should have a BIG influence over the types of metals that you buy.

Bullion That Can Be Sold Privately

Selling back your precious metals is a bit more involved than buying them. That's why in the beginning I stressed how important it is that you plan your exit strategy in advance. You'll see why in a moment.

This is the key part that separates the PRIVATE transactions from the NON-PRIVATE transactions. The important factors are; what types of items you are selling back and what quantity of items are you selling back. Privacy factors come down to what you have to sell, and how much of it that you have to sell. Certain types of transactions are required by US Law to be reported to the IRS by the broker/dealer whom you sell your metals back to.

The IRS has a form titled 1099-B. You can view a sample of this from in the Forms Chapter. If you are selling back certain types of gold and silver and/or certain quantities of gold and silver, the broker/dealer that you sell to is required to complete an IRS Form 1099-B that reports the **sale** of your metals. They also must send a copy of that same form to the Internal Revenue Service (IRS). Obviously when you have to report the sale of your metals to the IRS, your privacy goes out the window.

Here are the two main questions a broker/dealer will ask you when you go to sell back your precious metals:

1. **What form of silver or gold bullion are you selling?** (In other words, what types of coins, bars, etc. are you selling?)

2. **What quantity of gold or silver bullion are you selling?** (This usually means how many coins or ounces are you selling and/or what weight of bars are you selling.)

Now, this brings us to the all-important question....

What Forms and Weights of Gold and Silver are <u>NOT</u> <u>Reportable</u> to the IRS in <u>ANY</u> Quantity When Sold?

Private Gold Bullion Coins

Below is a list of some of the most widely known and commonly sold gold bullion coins that are *private*. (There are some other less popular coins that are also private that do not appear on this list. The scope of this book is geared towards the most common, popular and widely available coins.) This list includes, but is not limited to, the following coins:

American Gold Eagle Coins in the following weights.

American Gold Eagle Coins

1 ounce   **½ ounce**   **¼ ounce**   **1/10 ounce**

American gold eagle coins are a great choice. They are produced by the US Mint and the United States Government guarantees the purity and weight of these coins. The gold eagle is probably the most recognized gold coin in the world and they are very easy to buy and sell. The most popular size is the 1 ounce size, but they also come in ½ ounce, ¼ ounce and even in 1/10 ounce sizes.

These American gold eagle coins are **NOT** reportable to the IRS when you **SELL** them in **ANY** quantity, in any face value of the coins, or any total in actual cash value. You can sell an **UNLIMITED** quantity of these coins and the sale of the metals is a PRIVATE, Non-Reportable event.

American Gold Buffalos and Gold Austrian Philharmonics

American Gold Buffalo

Gold Austrian Philharmonics

The American Gold Buffalo coins are only available in a 1 ounce size.

The Gold Austrian Philharmonics are available in 1 ounce, ½ ounce, ¼ ounce and 1/10 ounce sizes. Both of these coins are popular, widely recognized and easily available. This makes them very easy to buy and sell.

When you sell ANY quantity of ANY sizes of these gold coins they are **NOT** Reportable to the IRS. You can sell an UNLIMITED quantity of any of these coins and the sale of the metals is a PRIVATE, Non-Reportable event.

Private Silver Bullion Coins

Below is a list of some of the most widely known and commonly sold silver bullion coins that are *private*. (There are some other less popular coins that are also private that do not appear on this list. The scope of this book is geared towards the most common, popular and widely available coins.) This list includes, but is not limited to, the following coins:

| American Sliver Eagle | Canadian Maple Leaf | Austrian Philharmonic |

These wonderful coins are available in 1 ounce weights only, (at the time of this writing). Each of these coins is minted and backed by their respective governments. The governments guarantee both the purity and the weights of these fine coins. All of these coins are very recognizable around the world and that makes them very easy to buy and sell.

These types of bullion coins are **<u>NOT</u>** Reportable to the IRS when you sell them in **ANY quantity**, any face value of the coins, or any total in actual cash value. You can sell an **UNLIMITED** quantity of these silver bullion coins and the sale of the metals is a PRIVATE, Non-Reportable event.

ALL of the above coins represent the most PRIVATE precious metals investments that can be made in the United States. Below is a summary of just what an excellent option these coins make for investors:

>You can BUY an UNLIMITED quantity of any of the above coins and the **PURCHASE** of these coins is NOT Reportable.

>If you buy the coins with a bank wire or check, or if you purchase less than $10,000 worth of these metals at a time with cash, the **TRANSACTION** is NOT Reportable.

>You can sell an unlimited quantity of these coins at any time and the **SALE** of the coins is NOT Reportable.

Folks, it just doesn't get any better than this!

Bullion That CANNOT Be Sold Privately

This area gets a little more complicated. Some of these items are reportable when you sell them and some are only reportable depending on how many you sell at one time. Below is a list of some of the most widely known and commonly sold bullion coins and bars that are either not private, or possibly private depending on the quantity you sell. This list includes, but is not limited to, the following coins and bars:

Non Private Gold Bullion

Gold Bullion Coins

| Canadian Maple Leaf | South African Krugerrand | Mexican Onza |

If you sell **25 or more** of the; 1 ounce Canadian Maple Leaf coins, 1 ounce South African Krugerrands or 1 ounce Mexican Onzas at one time, **it IS a Reportable event.**

The broker/dealer who is buying the coins from you will be required to complete IRS form 1099-B. They will send you an IRS Form 1099-B that reports the sale of your metals. They also will send a copy of that same form to the Internal Revenue Service (IRS). Obviously when you have to report the sale of your metals, your transaction is no longer private.

The 1099-B form requires reporting the seller's full name, address, social security number, etc. Sure, the IRS already has your information but your metals broker probably did not already have it. A lot of people are extremely cautious about giving out this information and want to do everything possible to limit it in every way.

You can sell **LESS** Than 25 of these coins at one time and the broker/dealer is **NOT** required to report the sale. When most people hear this they quickly think to themselves, no problem, I will just sell 24 coins today, and 24 more coins tomorrow or a week, and I will escape the reporting issue. Good try, but no cigar. Broker/dealers are required by law to report related transactions like this.

The IRS takes these requirements very seriously. They warn dealers against customers trying to evade their obligations by dividing up their sales into smaller units. In fact, the wording is; *"Sales of precious metals for a single customer during a 24-hour period must be aggregated and treated as a single sale."* And even the time limit does not hold up where, *"The broker knows or has reason to know that a customer, either alone or with a related person, is engaging in sales to avoid information reporting."*

When sellers get creative by attempting to sell bullion in multiple transactions to try and skirt the reporting requirements, these actions may expose the seller to further scrutiny and possible prosecution. A dealer that determines that a seller is using a pattern of sales to avoid 1099-B reporting is required to file a Suspicious Activity Report (SAR).

Here's something important to think about.

Some of you reading this may be thinking to yourself, no problem. What's the rush? If I need to space out the selling of my gold coins over a longer period of time to avoid having to report the sale, it's no big deal. I'll just sell some here… wait a while, and then sell some there, and I'll be just fine. Yes, you can do that and if it works out like that, then you will be fine. However, it's very important that you consider this. Keep in mind that the metals markets can often move very, very quickly. Sometimes at lightning speed!

As the global economy becomes more and more unstable, it's very likely that the swings in metals prices will become more dramatic. If for any reason gold or silver were to dramatically spike up in price, many people would want to take advantage of the price serge and liquidate at the top, right? To avoid reporting, if you have to sell off a little here, wait a while and then sell a little there, it's possible that you could miss the best selling opportunity due to you having to wait to fully cash out. Sometimes prices can fall sharply after a big run-up in price. You should at least plan for this and make it part of your purchasing strategy. This is more like the strategy of chess, than just a game of checkers.

Gold Bullion Bars

When selling any types of gold bars, if your sales transaction involves 1 Kilo (32.15 troy ounces) or more of .995 (or greater) fineness gold, the transaction **IS** a reportable event and the 1099-B form must be completed and sent to the IRS. This would include the sale of one, 1 Kilo bar or any number of smaller weight bars whose totals add up to 1 or more Kilos in weight.

It does not matter if you have generic gold bars or if you have name brand gold bars, the reporting requirement is based on the weight, not the brand of the gold bar(s). And just as mentioned above, it's not smart to try and play games and sell 30 ounces today and another 28 ounces in a few days, just to try and stay under the limit.

Privately Minted Gold Bars

Above are some examples of privately minted gold bars. Keep in mind, just because these are Privately Minted bars, if you sell 1 Kilo or more of them at one time, your sales transaction will become **NON-PRIVATE** and will be reported to the government.

If you sell **LESS** than 1 Kilo at a time, then the sales transaction is **NOT Reportable** and you will be fine. You just need to make sure there is enough time between your various sales transactions if you intend to sell more than 1 Kilo and don't want the transaction to be reported.

Silver Bullion
Rounds and Silver Bars

In case you do not know, a silver round is the common name that's used to describe a silver coin that is produced by a private mint. Rounds are not produced by Government Mints and the weight and purity of the coins are not guaranteed by a Government.

If you sell 1,000 ounces or more of silver bullion rounds and/or silver bars that are .999 fine silver, at any one time, it **IS** a Reportable event. This list includes, but is not limited to, the following coins and bars.

All types of silver rounds, 1,000 oz bars, 100 oz bars, 10 oz bars and 1 oz bars, etc. As long as the total weight of the silver items you are selling totals 1,000 ounces or more with any one sales transaction, the sale **IS** reportable and a 1099-B form must be completed and sent to the IRS. And as you now know, your privacy with a transaction like this goes away.

However, you can sell **LESS** than 1,000 ounces at one time of these types of silver bullion items and it will **NOT** be a reportable transaction. Below is an example of some types of silver bullion rounds and bars that are applicable.

Silver Rounds and .999 Fine Silver Bars

Junk Silver

Junk silver is a term used to describe most silver coins produced by Governments mainly to be used as legal tender. The coins are usually in fair condition but have no numismatic or collectible value above the bullion content value of the silver that the coin contains. The most common forms of junk silver in the US are pre 1965 US dimes, quarters, half dollars, etc. that were made of 90% actual silver. You typically buy $1,000 face value bags, or $500, $250, $100 face value bags of these coins. The face value simply means that, if you count up the face amount of each coin in the bag, like $.10 here and $.50 there, the total amount would be the face value. Don't confuse the face value with the actual market value of junk silver. For example, at the time of this writing, a $1,000 face value bag of junk silver is worth almost $20,000.

If you sell a $1,000 face value bag or more, in any one transaction, then it **IS** a reportable event and you will have to complete the 1099-B form, etc.

If you sell LESS than a $1,000 face value worth of 90% junk silver coins, then it is NOT a reportable event.

Above is a picture of a bag of junk silver. Keep in mind that these coins are still US legal tender and you could spend these coins just as you would with our current dated coins, but since the silver content makes these coins so much more valuable, that would not be a wise thing to do.

Platinum and Palladium

Even though platinum and palladium are not anywhere near as popular investment metals as gold and silver, they still have their rules and requirements because they are considered precious metals.

When you sell Platinum bars in quantities of 25 ounces or more in one transaction, it **IS** a reportable event. You can sell LESS than 25 ounces of these metals and the transaction will be exempt from reporting.

When you sell Palladium bars in quantities of 100 ounces or more in one transaction, it **IS** a reportable event. You can sell LESS than 100 ounces of these metals and the transaction will be exempt from reporting.

As far as the coins go, platinum bullion coins like the U.S. Platinum Eagle, the platinum Canadian Maple Leaf and the platinum Australian Koala are exempt from reporting when sold in ANY quantities.

Additionally, palladium bullion coins like the Canadian Palladium Maple Leaf and the Russian Ballerina are exempt from reporting when sold in ANY quantities.

Reporting Your Capital Gains Taxes

If you are like most precious metals investors, at some point in time you will likely want to sell some or all of your holding and hopefully make a big, fat, profit. And if you do make a profit, you can be sure that Uncle Sam will be right there with you looking to get his share of your profits. Even though you may have bought the right coins and kept your purchases private, and even though you may have sold the right coins and kept the actual sale of your metals private, you still have you pay income taxes on your gain. If on the other hand, you unfortunately lose money, you will be able to deduct the loss on your income taxes.

It's important to remember that it is up to YOU to report your capital gains on your tax returns. It is NOT up to the broker/dealer whom you sold your metals to. They most likely have no idea what you paid for the metals when you bought them and it's not their responsibility to report your capital gains earnings to the IRS.

Here is some great news! You never have any capital gains or losses until you actually SELL your precious metals. You can hold on to your metals for decades. You can cycle through huge "paper" gains and huge "paper" losses during that time. But it is not until you actually sell them, that you then realize a gain or a loss.

Profit and Loss on Your Precious Metals

Before you are able to determine the income tax consequences from selling your metals, you have to determine how much you made or lost. You first need to determine your total cost basis of your metals. This should include the total amount you spent to buy the metals. Don't forget to include all of the fees that you paid when you made your purchase such as shipping, commissions, payment costs, etc. Also, if you paid any storage fees for your metals, that is a valid costs and should be added to your total cost basis.

Next, you simply subtract your total cost basis from the total net amount you received when you sold your bullion. If the number is positive, then congratulations, you have a capital gain. If it is a negative amount, then unfortunately you lost money. It's that simple.

How Do You Determine Your Tax Rates

The key here is, how long have you owned the precious metals that you bought? If you have owned them for one year or less and you have a gain, then it is considered a short-term gain and is taxed as ordinary income. If you held your metals for more than a year and have a gain, then it's considered a long-term capital gain and you are taxed at the current long-term capital gains rate.

You can use a loss to offset your like gains. You offset long-term capital gains with long-term capital losses and you offset short-term capital gains with short-term capital losses. If your losses happen to completely offset your capital gains, you can usually use any leftover losses to offset other income.

As of this writing, according to the tax code, gold, silver, and platinum bullion are treated as collectibles. That means that your gains are usually treated as income. If you have a long-term gain it gets reported on the 1040 Schedule D.

Note, you may need to file estimated taxes after you sell bullion. This is typically the case if you end up owing the IRS at least $1,000 after withholdings are accounted for.

As I am sure you know, tax laws change all the time. The current tax law may be completely different from the information contained in this book due to a change since this book was written. The author is neither a CPA nor a tax advisor and does not attempt to give tax advice. It is always strongly recommended that you seek the advice of an experienced and competent tax advisor before making any investment and/or tax related decisions.

Formulating Your Plan of Action

Now that you have had a chance to review all of the options and pros and cons of these choices, it should be much easier for you to construct a precious metals investing plan that perfectly suits your needs. By now you may have your mind made up and know exactly what you want to do. Congratulations. Or, you may still be evaluating your options. If that's the case, here's some information that you may find helpful.

People often call me with questions about precious metals strategies and I try and help them to think it through and come up with the solution that best meets their individual needs. Of all of the different investment strategies, ideas and concepts that I have heard, here is one thing that I do know for sure and I think it's wise to consider.

What I know for sure is that absolutely no one knows what the future holds. We are living in unprecedented times and navigating in uncharted waters. The GDP of the USA is higher than any country has ever reached since the beginning of time. The level of debt that we have is also unprecedented.

As I am writing this, our Government is printing and/or creating 85 Billion new dollars per month! If they continue at this pace, in just 12 short months they will have printed/created an additional Trillion dollars in just one year. In the beginning it took our government about 95 years to print that much money and now we are printing that much in a single year. Do you think there is a chance that all of this out-of-control printing of dollars is going to dilute your paper fiat dollars and possibly your life savings?

You can use all of the formulas and projections you want, but how all of this is going to play out is really unknown. In my personal opinion, I think we are in for some very difficult economic times ahead and if you do nothing to prepare for that possibility, I think it's simply short-sighted and unwise. After all, the *"writing on the wall"* has never been clearer.

So given the above, logic and sound problem solving tells me that since there are so many <u>unknowns</u> looking into the future, it just makes good since to go with all of the "<u>knowns</u>" that we have right now. The "knowns" that we have right now are, at this current time, there are certain precious metals listed above that are not reportable to the government and are thus "Private." Could that change? Absolutely. However, it may not.

I get questions like this all of the time:

<>Do you think the government will ever forcibly confiscate our gold and/or silver?

<>Do you think the government will dramatically raise the capital gains tax on precious metals to discourage metals investing?

<>Do you think the government will ever make the purchase of gold and silver illegal?

<>Do you think the government will ever force us to "turn in" our precious metals?

The questions go on and on. I'm sure you notice the common element in all of the above questions, right? It's "The Government." Everyone is concerned about what the Government may or may not do. I can tell you this, the Government can do anything they darn well please, at any time they please, so you can't assume anything these days.

I'm not at all advocating that anyone become a hermit and go live in a cave. I think we should live each day to its fullest with optimism and hope, and always expect things to get better. However, in my personal opinion I think it just makes all of the since in the world to do whatever you can to limit the Government's involvement in your life and your financial affairs, because you never know.

If the government is now basically telling us…*"You can buy all of these certain types of gold and silver coins you want… and if you don't buy too much of them with paper dollars… you do not have to report your purchases…. And you can sell all of them that you want… at any time that you want… and if you sell the right ones, in the right amounts, you don't have to report the sale of those gold and silver coins to us either."* … then I think it's crazy not to take advantage of that.

With that being said, I think it is a total *no-brainer* not to at least put a hefty amount of your metals portfolio into the "Private" options stated above.

If you go back and look at price charts of gold and silver, you will clearly see that they all have big spikes in prices from time to time, and those spikes don't last forever. They go up, and they go down. The ideal situation would obviously be to sell at the top of the price cycle. Predicting the top of the price cycle is very difficult, or impossible to do. However, we do know that typically price peeks do not last very long.

So given this, if keeping your metals investments private is important to you, why would you buy large quantities of non-private metals that would limit your ability to sell them in the quantities you need to, at the time you need to, privately? If you have to spread the sales of your metals out over a period of time to keep them "un-reportable", you will most likely miss the best-selling time-period.

Another interesting thing to consider is this. As "interesting" developments continue to unfold with our Government, foreign Governments and the global economy; it's quite possible that the premiums on the *"private"* metals listed above could increase a great deal. That just seems very likely to me. It's all about supply and demand.

It is estimated that approximately 2% of all Americans today own some amount of physical gold and silver bullion. At the time I am writing this, the US Mint has run out of silver eagle coins several times in the last few months. They have also recently broken their all-time production and sales records as they struggle to keep up with the ever growing demand. So here are two questions to think about;

1. What do you think would happen to the supply and the price of precious metals if the percentage of Americans owning metals increased by just 1%?

2. As these first-time metals buyers flood into the market because they are concerned about the continued devaluation of the dollar, and as our Government continues to grow out of control, raise taxes, erode our privacy and chip away at our freedoms, do you think most of these people will choose to buy "private" metals or "non-private" metals?

Call me crazy, but my guess is that the demand for the *"private"* metals is going to soar. If this happens, it will make those metals super easy to sell, and they will likely carry higher sales premiums due to the heightened demand for them.

I realize that everyone has their own beliefs and motivations. Not everyone, I guess, is interested in privacy. So at the end of the day you should clearly make the decisions that are best for you and your family. Whatever you decide to purchase, the important thing is that you take action. I encourage you not to sit on the sidelines and over annualize this. Owning some metals, even if they may not be the right metals, is far better than not owning any at all.

Thanks so much for reading this book. I sincerely hope that this information has been enlightening and valuable to you. I know it can make a positive impact in your precious metals investing.

Please be sure to review the valuable **Resources** below.

Wishing you the very best in your precious metals investing and please remember to keep gold and silver in the proper perspective in your life.

Thanks so much and God Bless.

Doyle Shuler

CEO, Multiple Streams Marketing, LLC

info@MultipleStreamsMarketing.com

Resources

I have been investing in precious metals for almost 30 years. Over that time, I've seen a lot of good things and regrettably, I've seen a lot of very, very bad things in the industry. I've seen people lose their life savings, and even seen some lose their homes, and the homes of their loved ones, by making really bad choices. In the early years, I had no one to guide me and steer me towards the good options. I had to learn by trial and error and believe me, there was lots of *"error"* and it always costs me dearly. It doesn't have to be that way for you.

Below are some resources that I think are excellent and believe you will find very helpful. In fact, I personally use all of these resources myself. Noted, I am an affiliate or owner of these items and should you decide to purchase any of them through my links, I will make a commission on them. However, my philosophy has always been to treat everyone as I would myself, so I *only* make available the resources that I truly believe are *"best in class"* and ones that offer excellent values.

Gold Silver Alliance

A lot of people ask me where I buy my gold and silver from. Over the years, I've made purchases from many, many different broker/dealers around the country, all with varying results. I've always wanted to have my own gold and silver company so I could do things the right way and treat people the way they deserve to be treated. I became so tired of all the games and shady sales tactics that far too many dealers use to take advantage of metals investors every day. Over the years, I've been fortunate to develop friendships with some really exceptional people who have top level connections with the largest metals wholesale suppliers in the world. We decided to form our own precious metals company that offers a new approach to metals investing.

We are a group of seasoned gold & silver professionals who believe in offering a fresh, new, bold approach to precious metals investing. The Gold Silver Alliance was formed to provide an easier and more affordable way for metals investors to buy and sell metals. The Alliance is a group of like-mined, value conscious, independent thinkers, who have the courage and wisdom to take the actions that are necessary to insure our own success.

You will love our Concierge Club. It's free to join and comes with tons of FREE member benefits. We treat our Concierge Club members the same way we like to be treated ourselves. We don't surprise you with hidden fees that pop-up out of nowhere. We don't bait-and-switch our members by luring them in with low advertised prices and then hard-sell them on items that are more profitable to us.

We operate with trust and integrity. It's who we are. Our philosophy is; *If we can offer our Alliance Members superb values and some of the smartest, seldom seen investment options on the planet, you will tell others about us and help us grow the Alliance.*

We offer value. We don't use high pressure, commissioned sales people. We don't spend millions on TV advertising and we don't pay movie stars to promote our company. We take those savings and funnel them back to our members in the form of more affordable prices. This allows us to offer our metals at prices that will make you smile. Our concierge associates will answer your questions and carefully guide you to the metals that are in your best interest and that offer the best values.

Our management team has over a half of century of experience in the precious metals industry. We have long standing relationships with some of the largest wholesale metals companies in the world. Due to our high level of metals purchases, we are able to purchase from our wholesalers at the lowest price levels they offer. That's how we provide value for our Alliance members.

Head over to GoldSilverAlliance.com right now. Sign up for free. Check out all the benefits that we give you for free, right off the bat. Check our LOW prices. We think you'll find them to be the lowest you will find. *You'll be glad you did.*

Barefoot Retirement Plan

You've probably heard of the old parable that talks about... *If you find something really good, you want to share it with your friends,* right? Well, that's how I feel about this program. This program is a true, **"Game Changer."** Once you understand just how unique and powerful it is, it truly has the ability to dramatically impact your life for the better! I share this with you for two important reasons.

First, this unique and *"little known"* program offers an optional way to buy precious metals, and earn market indexed returns on the same funds you used to purchase your metals, at the same time. It's a unique way to use arbitrage, and "double dip" on your earnings, and really maximize your investment returns. Really amazing.

Second, it's one of the finest retirement programs ever created by man. No exaggeration. In fact, this is a relatively new (less than a year old), **patented program,** and it can only be offered by a very small number of select few experts. The actual concept has been used for over 150 years. This patented version of the program, reduces its cost by up to 70%, and makes it one of the best retirement options ever created.

Did you know that in a recent study, it was determined that 61% of Americans fear running out of money during retirement, more than they fear death itself? Plus, 87% of Americans are not confidant that they have saved enough for retirement! Man, those stats really shocked me, but they're true. And with all of the crazy ups & downs in the economy, our raging debt crisis, the health care debacle, global unrest, etc., it's easy to see why people are so frightened about this. After all, who wants to spend their retirement years as a Walmart greeter, right?

Here's the thing. This program is definitely not for everybody. It may not be your cup of tea, or you may not even qualify to participate in it, but I can certainly tell you this. Some of the wealthiest people in the country, and many of the largest companies in the country, are participating in this program in a BIG way because of the amazing value and benefits it offers. Some companies are literally putting tens of billions of dollars into programs like this.

In other words, if it was not such a fabulous program, these individuals and companies would certainly not be falling over themselves to take advantage of it. Of all the investment and retirement programs I have ever seen, in my entire life, this one is hands down, miles ahead of anything else out there! The benefits it offers are nothing short of *jaw-dropping!*

<u>Here are just some of the benefits this amazing program offers</u>: **100% Tax-Free income, guaranteed not to lose a penny due to market downturns, completely and totally private, can offer a life-time income, no contribution limits, one of the safest programs on planet earth, liquid and flexible, option to leverage and earn two different returns on the exact same funds, no investment restrictions, the lowest fees found anywhere.**

Yep... I told you it was really amazing. And these are not even all of the benefits that the program offers.

If this sounds like something you would like to find out more about, we've put together an outstanding book that will show you exactly how it works, why it's so different from anything else out there, and how it may dramatically benefit you, your family, your business, and your loved ones.

You can purchase the book at just about any online store. However, for a limited-time, we are making the eBook version of the book available *Totally Free!* I honestly don't know how long we will be able to continue making it free, but at the time of this writing, the book is totally and completely free on the website.

To grab your *FREE COPY* of The Barefoot Retirement Plan, go to:

www.BarefootRetirement.com

You'll be glad you did!

Plus, we are offering a
100% FREE Retirement CheckUP.

Similar retirement checkups cost $500 or more. **Ours is completely Free.** This is one of the finest retirement checkups on the market. It only takes a few minutes to enter in your information. You will receive a 17 page detailed report with color charts & graphs that will clearly show you if you're on track to reach your retirement goals.

Why worry about what your retirement will look like when you can find out for sure, in just a few minutes. And it won't cost you a cent.

To get your Retirement CheckUP while it's still 100% FREE, go to:

BarefootRetirement.com/CheckUP

SurvivalResources.org

I am fortunate to have quite a few high net worth friends. Want to know something that just about all of them have in common? They all have stocked up like crazy on survival resources of all types (including metals). These are not the crazy people you see on TV that live in the woods and are dooms day freaks.

These are multi-millionaires who can afford just about anything they want. They're smart people. They know that smart people have contingency PLANS. They plan for the worst, just in case it happens, so they will be prepared. They look at survival preparedness like they look at buying insurance. Prudent people buy insurance to protect themselves from the unexpected.

Anyone who is half-way paying attention to what's going on these days knows that we are truly living in unprecedented times. Things are happening today that none of us would have ever imagined just a hand full of years ago. So smart people prepare for the unexpected.

A buddy of mine is friends with a former Navy Seal. This guy lives and breathes survival preparedness and boy does he know his stuff. He recently spent several hours reviewing and demonstrating the core survival items that he deems as critical, must-have items. I was so impressed (and shocked) by what he had to say, I decided to create a website that contains all of the survival items he and other experts rely on themselves.

The site is: SurvivalResources.org There you will find all of his recommended items, all in one place. You won't have to scour the web and spend endless hours trying to figure out what's good and what is not. It's all here on this one site. It's like a one-stop-shop site, for all of the *"Navy Seal Recommended"* survival items you need. Check it out today. Be sure you and your family are fully prepared for the unexpected. Note; once you stock up on these items, you can't imagine how much better you will sleep at night.

Easy IRA Solutions

If you've not put at least some of your IRA or 401K funds into a physical gold and silver IRA and/or 401K, you are missing out on one of the best opportunities you will ever have in your lifetime! Many financial planners are now suggesting investors put 10% to 30% of their investment portfolio in physical gold and silver. There are only a handful of companies that allow you to have **physical gold and silver** in your IRA account.

Mainly there are two different types of self-directed IRA platforms, the **Trust model** and the **Checkbook Control model**. The huge majority of "Gold IRA" programs that you see advertised are based on the Trust model. The **Trust model** allows the companies to charge a ton of fees. Fees like managerial fees, transaction fees, annual asset fees, wire fees, entrance and exit fees, purchase and sell fees, holding fees and much more.

It's not uncommon to have to pay thousands of dollars in fees, PER YEAR, on your *"free"* gold IRA. Plus, in addition to that, many of these Trust model companies dictate **where you buy** your metals from and dictate **where you store** your metals. And guess what, they often earn fees when you buy your metals and every month when you pay to store your metals. If you like paying never-ending fees, you will love the Trust model.

Thankfully there is a better way. The **Self-Directed IRA** based on the **Checkbook Control model** offers much, much more flexibility. Plus, there are no managerial or transaction fees. This model allows you to purchase your metals from anyone you choose. Another big thing to consider is most IRA *"require"* you to store your metals in licensed depositories and many IRA custodians earn commissions on your storage fees forever. With the IRA program I found, they have the customer's best interest in mind and educate them about the fact that, if you purchase the right, Government IRA approved coins, the tax code does NOT place any restrictions whatsoever on the storage requirements for them. Based on the tax law, your IRA can purchase certain gold and silver coins and you can store them personally. This is a big, big deal and you can save a lot of money with this option if it's right for you.

The Self-Directed IRA allows you to shop around and find best prices for your metals and for your storage, if you choose to. Another thing I totally love about the Checkbook Control model is that after you buy as much gold and silver as you deem sound for your portfolio, you can also invest in things like; residential and commercial real estate, raw land, trust deeds and mortgages, private notes and placements, LLCs, foreclosure property, receivables, stocks, bonds, mutual funds, currency, futures, commercial paper and much, much more. This puts the power and flexibility into your hands and allows you to invest in the best opportunities and in what you know best. You can't believe how easy it is. When you want to buy an approved asset in your IRA, you simply write the check. That's it. Hence the name, checkbook IRA.

Many investors these days want to invest in gold and silver but they are cash poor. They don't have a lot of liquid money sitting around to buy much metals with. However, most people do have a sizable IRAs and/or 401ks that they could buy the precious metals they want, if they structure a new precious metals IRA correctly.

To find out more about how this unique and very profitable program works, go to: www.EasyIRASolutions.com

---

Where Should I Store My Precious Metals?

(**Note:** As an author, public personality and spokesperson on precious metals, I DO NOT keep any precious at my residence or office. All of my metals at stored at non-disclosed, off site vault storage locations.)

This is a question I get several times a week. It's not uncommon to have new metals investors buy 50K, 100K or several hundred thousand dollars right off the bat. Yes, there are a lot of people, buying LOTS of metals these days.

Lots of new investors have no idea of where or how to safely store the metals they buy. I have spent hundreds of hours talking with people about the multitude of options for storing their metals and the pros and cons of them. You probably guessed it by now, but I finally grew tired of spending so much of my time explaining this to people, so I wrote a book on the subject.

It's actually a BEST SELLER and I believe it's the most comprehensive book on the subject of storing precious metals that you will find anywhere. The book is available online. It's very inexpensive and I promise you will learn things about storing metals that you have never imagined before. And…since the safety issue is so big with gold and silver, this could be the most important book about metals that you ever read. Seriously. This subject is nothing to take lightly.

You can check it out by going to:

http://safelink8.com/StorageBook

Forms

Here is a screen shot of IRS Form 1099-B. This is the from that will need to be completed and sent to the IRS each time you sell any precious metals that are required to be reported when sold. This form is required for all "non-private" precious metals sales.

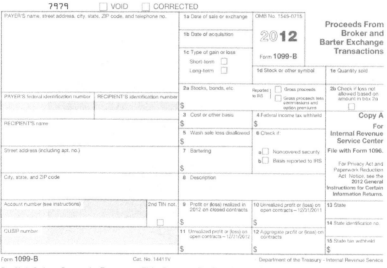

Here are some screen shots of IRS From 8300. This is the form that must be completed and returned to the IRS when any CASH purchases are made in the amount of $10,000 or more.

IRS Form 8300 (Rev. July 2012)
OMB No. 1545-0892
Department of the Treasury
Internal Revenue Service

Report of Cash Payments Over $10,000 Received in a Trade or Business
► See instructions for definition of cash.
► Use this form for transactions occurring after July 8, 2012. Do not use prior versions after this date.
For Privacy Act and Paperwork Reduction Act Notice, see the last page.

FinCEN Form 8300 (Rev. July 2012)
OMB No. 1506-0018
Department of the Treasury
Financial Crimes Enforcement Network

1 Check appropriate box(es) if: a ☐ Amends prior report;   b ☐ Suspicious transaction.

Part I Identity of Individual From Whom the Cash Was Received

2 If more than one individual is involved, check here and see instructions . . . . ►

3 Last name	4 First name	5 M.I.	6 Taxpayer identification number

7 Address (number, street, and apt. or suite no.)	8 Date of birth (see instructions) ► M M D D Y Y Y Y

9 City	10 State	11 ZIP code	12 Country (if not U.S.)	13 Occupation, profession, or business

14 Identifying document (ID)	a Describe ID ► c Number ►	b Issued by ►

Part II Person on Whose Behalf This Transaction Was Conducted

15 If this transaction was conducted on behalf of more than one person, check here and see instructions . . . . ►

16 Individual's last name or organization's name	17 First name	18 M.I.	19 Taxpayer identification number

20 Doing business as (DBA) name (see instructions)	Employer identification number

21 Address (number, street, and apt. or suite no.)	22 Occupation, profession, or business

23 City	24 State	25 ZIP code	26 Country (if not U.S.)

27 Alien identification (ID)	a Describe ID ► c Number ►	b Issued by ►

Part III Description of Transaction and Method of Payment

28 Date cash received M M D D Y Y Y Y	29 Total cash received $ .00	30 If cash was received in more than one payment, check here . . ► ☐	31 Total price if different from item 29 $ .00

32 Amount of cash received (in U.S. dollar equivalent) (must equal item 29) (see instructions):

a U.S. currency $_____ .00 (Amount in $100 bills or higher $_____ .00)
b Foreign currency $_____ .00 (Country ►_____)
c Cashier's check(s) $_____ .00   Issuer's name(s) and serial number(s) of the monetary instrument(s) ►
d Money order(s) $_____ .00
e Bank draft(s) $_____ .00
f Traveler's check(s) $_____ .00

33 Type of transaction
a ☐ Personal property purchased
b ☐ Real property purchased
c ☐ Personal services provided
d ☐ Business services provided
e ☐ Intangible property purchased
f ☐ Debt obligations paid
g ☐ Exchange of cash
h ☐ Escrow or trust funds
i ☐ Bail received by court clerks
j ☐ Other (specify in item 34) ►

34 Specific description of property or service shown in 33. Give serial or registration number, address, docket number, etc. ►

Part IV Business That Received Cash

Part IV Business That Received Cash

35 Name of business that received cash	36 Employer identification number

37 Address (number, street, and apt. or suite no.)	Social security number

38 City	39 State	40 ZIP code	41 Nature of your business

42 Under penalties of perjury, I declare that to the best of my knowledge the information I have furnished above is true, correct, and complete.

Signature ► _____ Authorized official   Title ► _____

43 Date of signature M M D D Y Y Y Y	44 Type or print name of contact person	45 Contact telephone number

IRS Form 8300 (Rev. 7-2012)   Cat. No. 62133S   FinCEN Form 8300 (Rev. 7-2012)

IRS Form 8300 (Rev. 7-2012)   Page 2   FinCEN Form 8300 (Rev. 7-2012)

Multiple Parties
(Complete applicable parts below if box 2 or 15 on page 1 is checked)

Part I Continued—Complete if box 2 on page 1 is checked

3 Last name			4 First name		5 M.I.	6 Taxpayer identification number
7 Address (number, street, and apt. or suite no.)				8 Date of birth (see instructions)		M M D D Y Y Y Y
9 City		10 State	11 ZIP code	12 Country (if not U.S.)	13 Occupation, profession, or business	
14 Identifying document (ID)	a Describe ID ▶ c Number ▶				b Issued by ▶	

3 Last name			4 First name		5 M.I.	6 Taxpayer identification number
7 Address (number, street, and apt. or suite no.)				8 Date of birth (see instructions)		M M D D Y Y Y Y
9 City		10 State	11 ZIP code	12 Country (if not U.S.)	13 Occupation, profession, or business	
14 Identifying document (ID)	a Describe ID ▶ c Number ▶				b Issued by ▶	

Part II Continued—Complete if box 15 on page 1 is checked

16 Individual's last name or organization's name		17 First name	18 M.I.	19 Taxpayer identification number
20 Doing business as (DBA) name (see instructions)				Employer identification number
21 Address (number, street, and apt. or suite no.)			22 Occupation, profession, or business	
23 City	24 State	25 ZIP code	26 Country (if not U.S.)	
27 Alien identification (ID)	a Describe ID ▶ c Number ▶		b Issued by ▶	

16 Individual's last name or organization's name		17 First name	18 M.I.	19 Taxpayer identification number
20 Doing business as (DBA) name (see instructions)				Employer identification number
21 Address (number, street, and apt. or suite no.)			22 Occupation, profession, or business	
23 City	24 State	25 ZIP code	26 Country (if not U.S.)	
27 Alien identification (ID)	a Describe ID ▶ c Number ▶		b Issued by ▶	

Comments – Please use the lines provided below to comment on or clarify any information you entered on any line in Parts I, II, III, and IV

58

Disclaimers

Disclaimer and Terms of Use Agreement

This book was designed to provide information about the subject matter covered herein. It is distributed with the understanding that the author and the publisher are not engaged in rendering financial, legal, accounting, or other professional services. If financial, legal accounting or other professional advice or other professional assistance is required, the services of a competent professional advisor should be sought.

Efforts have been made to make this book as complete and accurate as possible. However, there may be mistakes both typographical and in content. Therefore, the texts should be used only as general guides and not as the ultimate sources of the subject matters covered.

The author and the publisher shall have neither liability nor responsibility to any person or entity with respect to any loss or damage caused or alleged to be caused directly or indirectly by the information covered in this report.

The author and publisher of this eBook, and the accompanying materials have used their best efforts in preparing this publication. The author and publisher make no representation or warranties with respect to the accuracy, applicability, fitness, or completeness of the contents of this book. The information contained in this book is strictly for educational purposes. Therefore, if you wish to apply any of the ideas contained in this book, you are taking full responsibility for your actions.

Every effort has been made to accurately represent this product and it's potential. Even though this industry is one that has a great upside profit potential, there is no guarantee that you will earn or save any money using the techniques and ideas contained in these materials. Examples in these materials are not to be interpreted as a promise or guarantee of earnings or savings. Earning and saving potential is entirely dependent on the person using this product and its ideas and techniques as well as market and economic conditions and fluctuations. We do not purport this as a get rich scheme. You could lose all of the money you invest in any investment. No one can predict the future nor market prices. You should only invest money that you can afford to lose and you should only invest after seeking council with your financial planner and/or advisor or other professionals in this field.

We cannot guarantee your success, savings or profits. Nor are we responsible for any of your actions.

Materials in our product and our websites may contain information that includes or is based upon forward-looking statements within the meaning or the securities litigation reform act of 1995. Forward-looking statements give our expectations or forecasts of future events. You can identify these statements by the fact that they do not relate strictly to historical or current facts. They use words such as "anticipate," "estimate," "expect," "project," "intend," "plan," "believe," and other words and terms of similar meaning in connection with a description of potential earnings or financial performance.

Any and all forward looking statements here or on any of our sales materials are intended to express our opinion of earnings or savings potential. Many factors will be important in determining your actual results and no guarantees are made that you will achieve results similar to ours or anybody else's, in fact no guarantees are made that you will achieve any results from our ideas and techniques in our materials.

The author and publisher disclaim any warranties (expressed or implied), merchantability, or fitness for any particular purpose. The author and publisher shall in no event be held liable to any party for any direct, indirect, punitive, special, incidental or other consequential damages arising directly or indirectly from any use of this material, which is provided "as is", and without warranties.

As always, the advice of a competent legal, financial, tax, accounting or other professional should be sought before taking any actions or making any purchases. The author and publisher do not warrant the performance, effectiveness or applicability of any sites listed or linked to in this book. All links are for information purposes only and are not warranted for content, accuracy or any other implied or explicit purpose.

any way other than what is outlined within this Book under any circumstances.

The End

Or Perhaps

The Beginning

Made in the USA
Columbia, SC
28 July 2019